The Power of Mental Transformation

How to change your thoughts and change your life.

Stephen William

Table of content

Chapter 1

Introduction: [*The importance of mental transformation*]

The importance of mental transformation cannot be overstated. Our minds are incredibly powerful, and the thoughts we have can shape our entire lives. If we are constantly thinking negative thoughts, we will attract negativity into our lives. On the other hand, if we focus on positivity and abundance, we will attract more positive experiences.

This is why it is so important to pay attention to our thoughts and make a conscious effort to transform them. It is not always easy, but it is possible. With practice and dedication, we can rewire our brains and create new thought patterns that serve us better.

Mental transformation can lead to a number of positive changes in our lives, including increased happiness, improved relationships, and greater success in our careers. By changing our thoughts, we can change our lives in profound ways. In this blog post, we will explore some strategies for transforming your thoughts and creating a more fulfilling life.

Our thoughts are incredibly powerful. They shape our perceptions, influence our emotions, and ultimately determine the actions we take. In other words, our thoughts are the foundation for every experience we have in life. The way we think about ourselves, others, and the world around us can either empower us or hold us back. It is essential to understand the power of our thoughts and how they shape our reality.

Negative thoughts can be particularly damaging. They can create self-doubt, anxiety, and depression. If we constantly think negative thoughts, we will attract negative experiences into our lives. On the other hand, positive thoughts can help us feel more confident, optimistic, and joyful. When we focus on positive thoughts, we attract positive experiences into our lives.

It's important to recognize that we have the power to change our thoughts. We can challenge negative beliefs and replace them with more positive ones. By doing so, we can transform our lives and create a more fulfilling and satisfying reality. It's not always easy, but with practice, we can learn to harness the power of our thoughts and use them to create the life we desire.

Chapter 3

How thoughts shape your life

Thoughts are incredibly powerful and can shape our lives in both positive and negative ways. They can influence our emotions, our behaviors, and our overall outlook on life. In fact, our thoughts can even impact our physical health.

Negative thoughts can lead to stress, anxiety, and depression, which can result in physical symptoms such as headaches, muscle tension, and fatigue. On the other hand, positive thoughts can lead to feelings of happiness, contentment, and fulfillment, which can improve our overall well-being and even boost our immune system.

It's important to recognize the power of our thoughts and how they impact our lives. If we constantly have negative thoughts, we'll attract negative experiences and people into our lives, which can lead to a downward spiral. On the other hand, if we focus on positive thoughts and visualize positive outcomes, we'll attract positive experiences and people into our lives, which can lead to an upward spiral of success and happiness.

Changing your thoughts can be difficult, but it's not impossible. It requires awareness, practice, and patience. Start by paying attention to your thoughts and identifying any negative patterns or self-talk. Once you're aware of these patterns, you can start to challenge them and replace them with positive thoughts and affirmations. Over time, this practice can lead to a complete transformation of your mindset and ultimately, your life.

Chapter 4

Identifying negative thinking patterns

Identifying negative thinking patterns is a crucial step in transforming your mental state. Negative thoughts are often automatic and can be hard to notice at first, but they can have a profound impact on your life. Some common negative thinking patterns include black-and-white thinking, catastrophizing, and personalization.

Black-and-white thinking is when you see things as either good or bad, with no in-between. This type of thinking can be very limiting and can prevent you from seeing the nuances of a situation. Catastrophizing is when you imagine the worst possible outcome for a situation, even if it's unlikely to happen. This type of thinking can cause unnecessary stress and anxiety. Personalization is when you take things personally that isn't actually about you. This type of thinking can lead to feelings of self-doubt and insecurity.

Once you've identified your negative thinking patterns, you can start to challenge them. One way to do this is to ask yourself if your thoughts are based in reality. Are you catastrophizing a situation that isn't actually that bad? Are you taking something personally that isn't actually about you? Another way to challenge negative thinking patterns is to reframe your thoughts in a more positive way. Instead of thinking, "I'm never going to be able to do this," try thinking, "I might struggle at first, but with practice, I can improve." Over time, these small changes in thinking can have a big impact on your mental state and your life as a whole.

Chapter 5

Techniques to change negative thinking patterns

Negative thinking patterns can have a significant impact on our lives. They can hold us back from achieving our goals and make us feel unhappy and dissatisfied. The good news is that it is possible to change these patterns and create a more positive outlook on life. Here are some techniques to help you change negative thinking patterns:

1. Identify negative thoughts: The first step towards changing negative thinking patterns is to identify them. Pay attention to your thoughts, and when you notice a negative thought, write it down.

2. Question negative thoughts: Once you have identified a negative thought, question its validity. Ask yourself if there is evidence to support it or if it is just a belief.

3. Reframe negative thoughts: Reframing negative thoughts involves turning them into positive ones. For example, instead of

thinking "I'm not good enough," reframe it as "I am capable of achieving my goals."

4. Practice gratitude: Practicing gratitude can help shift your focus from negative thoughts to positive ones. Take time each day to reflect on the things you are grateful for.

5. Surround yourself with positivity: Surround yourself with positive people, read positive books, and listen to uplifting music. The more positivity you surround yourself with, the easier it will be to change negative thinking patterns.

By using these techniques, you can transform your negative thinking patterns and create a more positive outlook on life. Remember, changing your thoughts can change your life.

Chapter 6

The power of positive affirmations

Positive affirmations are powerful tools for transforming negative thoughts and promoting positive change in our lives. These are positive statements that we repeat to ourselves to counteract negative thoughts and beliefs.

Affirmations can be used to target any area of our lives where we feel we need improvement, whether it's confidence, self-esteem, relationships, health, or career success. By focusing on positive affirmations, we can reprogram our minds to believe in positive outcomes and possibilities.

To begin using affirmations, start by identifying a specific area of your life that you'd like to work on. Then, create a positive statement that relates to that area. For example, if you want to improve your confidence, you could repeat the affirmation "I am confident and capable" to yourself throughout the day.

It's important to repeat affirmations consistently over time to see positive results. Try incorporating affirmations into your morning routine or writing them down and keeping them somewhere you'll see them often.

While positive affirmations can be powerful, it's important to note that they are not a substitute for taking action. Affirmations work best when they are paired with action steps towards achieving our goals.

Incorporating positive affirmations into our daily routine is a simple yet effective way to shift our mindset and transform our lives.

Chapter 7

How to create a positive mindset

Creating a positive mindset can be extremely powerful in transforming your life. It's not always easy, but it's definitely worth the effort. Here are a few tips to help you create a more positive mindset:

1) Practice gratitude: Focus on what you have, rather than what you lack. Take a few minutes each day to think about the things in your life that you're grateful for, no matter how big or small they may be.

2) Surround yourself with positivity: Spend time with people who uplift you and make you feel good about yourself. Avoid negative people who bring you down and drain your energy.

3) Replace negative self-talk with positive affirmations: We all have an inner critic that tells us we're not good enough. Learn to recognize these negative thoughts and replace them with positive

affirmations. For example, instead of saying "I can't do this," say "I am capable and I will succeed."

4) Focus on solutions, not problems: Instead of dwelling on problems, focus on finding solutions. This will help you feel more empowered and in control of your life.

5) Take care of yourself: Practice self-care by getting enough sleep, eating healthy and exercising regularly. When you feel good physically, it's easier to maintain a positive mindset.

By incorporating these habits into your daily routine, you can create a more positive mindset and transform your life for the better. Remember, changing your thoughts can change your life!

Chapter 8

The role of gratitude in mental transformation

Gratitude is a powerful tool in mental transformation. It is about being thankful for what you have and focusing on the positives in your life. When you practice gratitude, you shift your focus from what you don't have to what you do have, and this can have a profound impact on your mental well-being.

Research has shown that practicing gratitude can lead to improved emotional and physical health, better sleep, increased self-esteem, and reduced stress levels. It can also help you develop a more positive outlook on life, improve your relationships, and increase your resilience in the face of challenges.

There are many ways to practice gratitude, such as keeping a gratitude journal, expressing gratitude to others, or simply taking a few moments each day to reflect on the things you are thankful for.

By incorporating gratitude into your daily routine, you can start to rewire your brain to focus on the positive aspects of your life and transform your mental state for the better.

Chapter 9

The impact of visualization on mental transformation

Visualization is a powerful tool that can help you achieve your goals by creating a mental picture of success. When you visualize yourself achieving your goals, you begin to believe that it's possible. This belief can then help to motivate you and keep you focused on your goals.

Visualization can be used in many different ways to help with mental transformation. One popular technique is to create a vision board. A vision board is a visual representation of your goals and aspirations. It can be a simple collage of images or a more elaborate display that includes words, phrases, and other visual cues.

Another way to use visualization is to create a mental movie. This technique involves imagining yourself achieving your goals in great detail. You can use all of your senses to make the experience as vivid as possible. Imagine the sights, sounds, and even the smells of success.

Visualization can also be used to help you overcome obstacles and challenges. By visualizing yourself overcoming these challenges, you can build up your confidence and resilience. This will help you to stay motivated and focused, even when the going gets tough.

In conclusion, visualization is a powerful tool that can help with mental transformation. By creating a mental picture of success, you can build up your confidence, stay motivated, and achieve your goals. So, take some time to visualize your goals and aspirations, and see how it can transform your life.

Chapter 10

The importance of self-care in mental transformation

Self-care is one of the most important aspects of mental transformation. It's important to take care of yourself physically, mentally, and emotionally. When you take care of yourself, you're better equipped to handle life's challenges, and you'll be more resilient when things do get tough.

Self-care can mean different things for different people. For some, it could be taking a long bath, going for a walk, cooking a healthy meal, or even just taking a few minutes to meditate or practice deep breathing exercises.

It's important to prioritize self-care and make it a part of your daily routine. It's easy to get caught up in the busyness of life and forget to take care of yourself, but doing so can lead to burnout and other negative consequences.

In addition to taking care of yourself physically, it's also important to take care of your mental and emotional health. This may involve seeking therapy or counseling, practicing mindfulness and meditation, or simply taking time for yourself to do the things you enjoy.

Remember, self-care isn't selfish, it's necessary. By taking care of yourself, you'll be better equipped to handle life's challenges and transform your thoughts and your life.

Chapter 11

Overcoming obstacles in mental transformation

Overcoming obstacles in mental transformation can be a difficult and often frustrating process. However, it is important to remember that progress is not always linear and setbacks are a natural part of the journey. Here are some tips to help you overcome obstacles in your mental transformation:

1. Identify the obstacle: The first step in overcoming any obstacle is to identify it. Take a moment to reflect on what is holding you back from achieving your mental transformation goals. Is it fear, self-doubt, or a lack of motivation?

2. Reframe negative thoughts: Once you have identified the obstacle, work on reframing any negative thoughts that might be contributing to it. For example, if you are experiencing self-doubt, try to focus on your strengths and accomplishments instead of your weaknesses.

3. Seek support: Don't be afraid to reach out for support from friends, family, or a mental health professional. Sometimes, talking through your obstacles with someone else can help you gain a new perspective and find solutions you might not have considered before.

4. Celebrate small victories: It is important to celebrate even small victories along the way. Recognize and celebrate progress, no matter how small, as a way to stay motivated and build momentum towards your mental transformation goals.

Remember, mental transformation is a journey, not a destination. Overcoming obstacles is a natural part of that journey, and with persistence and patience, you can achieve your goals and change your life for the better.

Chapter 12

The benefits of mental transformation

Mental transformation is a powerful tool that can change your life in many ways. One of the main benefits of mental transformation is the ability to change your negative thoughts into positive ones. Negative thoughts can hold you back from achieving your goals and can even lead to depression and anxiety. By transforming your negative thoughts into positive ones, you can improve your mood, increase your motivation, and achieve your goals with ease.

Another benefit of mental transformation is the ability to improve your relationships with others. By changing your perspective and focusing on the positive aspects of a situation, you can improve your communication skills and build stronger relationships with those around you.

Mental transformation can also help you to become more resilient and adaptable. Life can be unpredictable, and unexpected challenges can arise at any time. By transforming your thoughts and focusing on the present moment, you can develop the skills needed to overcome obstacles and bounce back from setbacks.

Finally, mental transformation can help you to live a more fulfilling life. By focusing on the positive aspects of life and embracing new challenges, you can develop a sense of purpose and meaning that will help you to live life to the fullest.

In conclusion, mental transformation is a powerful tool that can improve your mood, strengthen your relationships, increase your resilience, and help you to live a more fulfilling life. By taking the time to transform your thoughts, you can unlock your full potential and achieve your goals with ease.

Starting your mental transformation journey can be daunting, but it's important to remember that it's a process and it takes time. Here are some key steps you can take to start your journey:

1. Identify your negative thoughts: Start by becoming aware of your negative thoughts and the impact they have on your life. Write them down and try to understand where they come from.

2. Challenge your negative thoughts: Once you have identified your negative thoughts, challenge them. Ask yourself if they are true, if there is evidence to support them, and if they are helping or hindering you.

3. Replace negative thoughts with positive ones: Once you have challenged your negative thoughts, replace them with positive ones. This can be as simple as reframing your thoughts in a more positive light.

4. Practice self-care: Take care of yourself both mentally and physically. This can include things like exercise, meditation, and spending time with loved ones.

5. Surround yourself with positivity: Surround yourself with positive people and positive environments. This can help to reinforce your new positive thoughts and beliefs.

Remember, changing your thoughts takes time and effort. But with practice and dedication, you can transform your mindset and change your life for the better.

Chapter 14

Conclusion:

The journey of mental transformation is worth it.

In conclusion, the journey of mental transformation is undoubtedly worth it. It may be a challenging journey, but the rewards are infinite. By changing your thoughts, you can change your life for the better. You can achieve your goals, improve your relationships, and become the best version of yourself.

The power of mental transformation lies within you. It all starts with a decision to take control of your thoughts and beliefs. You have the power to choose your thoughts and direct your focus. It is essential to surround yourself with positive influences, such as supportive people or inspiring content, to help you maintain a positive mindset.

Remember that mental transformation is not an overnight process. It takes time, effort, and patience to develop new habits and beliefs.

However, with consistency and determination, you can achieve the transformation you desire.

In conclusion, mental transformation is a journey that requires self-awareness, positive thinking, and consistent effort. It is a journey that is worth taking because it can lead to a fulfilling and satisfying life. So, take the first step towards mental transformation today and watch your life transform.

I hope this book has provided you with valuable insight on how to change your thoughts and transform your life. It's amazing to think about the power of our thoughts and how they can shape our reality. By making a conscious effort to shift negative thinking patterns and cultivate positive ones, you can experience a significant transformation in your life. Remember, change takes time and effort, so be patient and kind to yourself as you embark on this journey. We believe in you and your ability to create a life that brings you happiness and fulfillment.